I0158357

solstice

solstice

laura lyrio caram

copyright © 2019 by laura lyrio caram.

all rights reserved. no part of this book may be
reproduced or used in any manner without written
permission of the copyright owner except for the use
of quotations in a book review.

definitions of winter and summer solstice were
extracted from britannica. the words on the back cover
were inspired by gary zukav's "solstice joy."

dedicated to my family
who lives beneath the arches
in green and orange
i love you

(an introduction)

write a letter to your future self explaining how to stop yourself from spiraling.

i look up and see her placing the pen into my palms.
i thought,
i thought,
and i thought.

i see myself in a building. i'm on ground zero. the parking lot feels scary and empty and the only light there is comes from the faint glow of the exit sign. the escape tempts me greatly. but i muster enough strength to venture on an expedition to find a staircase. and then it's all about climbing and letting it hurt and feeling my heart drop as i pant and shout that i'm tired and can't do it and i'm not enough and it would be so much easier to just stop and let go of the railings. yet... i push through the pain.

where are you now?

my muscles cramp and i allow my eyes to flutter open and watch my chest rise and fall and rise and fall. i stare at the planets and stars in awe and wonder. i take the time to contemplate the world we live in and the universe surrounding us and think about what i've gone through and what i'm going through and the way life turns out and why things work the way they do. and i have so much more to go through. to live through. but oh how beautiful it will be when i get there.

table of contents

winter solstice

"the sun travels the shortest path through the sky, and that day therefore has the least daylight and the longest night"

laura lyrio

there has been a great deal of loneliness in my life
i now welcome it as i would an old friend
it strangles me with its truth
and captivates me with its substance
how can loneliness be lonely
if it never stops chasing me?

(whispers)

solstice

i am wedged between romance and fiction
with my legs beneath my chin
weeping so softly
so as to not disturb those temporarily engulfed
in another universe
(any is far greater than this one)
and i do not tell anybody

what is the point?

laura lyrio

sophomore year
we watched spoken word
about a girl who could never love herself
easy i thought
so i came home that day
stood in front of the mirror
ready to say *i love you* to my reflection
i couldn't and cried

(when i realized things had to change)

solstice

would you be happy
if you lived alone
in a world with just
you?

tell me again
how my happiness
solely
relies on myself

(contributing factors)

my life shakes in accordance with every muscle's tremble
my mouth is unwilling to decide whether it prefers to
open or close
no words could force themselves past the sporadic barrier
with every groan that managed to slip past
like a ripple a tear would follow
and so i called the only friend i knew would
understand without understanding
life will consume you if you take it all at once
trust me i know
take every individual hardship
with three good things
and i know it will be hard
but it's what you have to do
and don't worry
i'll bring you cookies tomorrow
i love you mi lara
i knew i would survive another day

(s)

solstice

what do you expect to gain
from this
she asked
the words hurt yet i let them
tumble

the ability to feel happy again

the reason it is so difficult for me to accept love
is because i have never had it in the first place
i deprive myself of affection
so that i may never be affected
my love language is built upon bitter words
and no effort to change

(i apologize for who i have become)

solstice

my first mistake
had the absolute power
to isolate me from the people i loved
the entirety of my body ached
after being forced to open up to countless people
each head count issued yet another invite to weakness
and so in tears my mother
left me in the hands of the only person
she entrusted to provide me guidance
but stepping out of that car
feelings of despondency and embarrassment
consumed me
this could not be real
yet my legs seemed to move on their own accord
and that is when
i saw vivid fire in the form of a person
her spark never dulled
her flames never stopped sparking

laura lyrio

she pulled out a chair meant for second
graders
(i did not mind for i felt smaller than them)
go into the pigsty and come out clean
she said
it is the only thing i carry with me now

(thank you mrs. valdes)

solstice

who shall i be today?

(social media personas)

laura lyrio

you tore your skin
to stitch your heart
you have created negation
within yourself

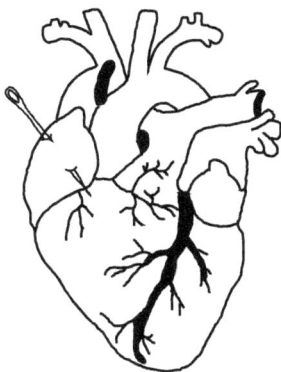

solstice

blood rushes to my face when i hear of people
complaining about their relatives for diminutive things
problems that aren't quite problems at all

my family lives an eight hour nine hundred dollar
plane ticket away
i would do anything
absolutely anything
every day for the rest of my life
for the chance to have them live near me

having a good family is a privilege
be thankful if you were granted one

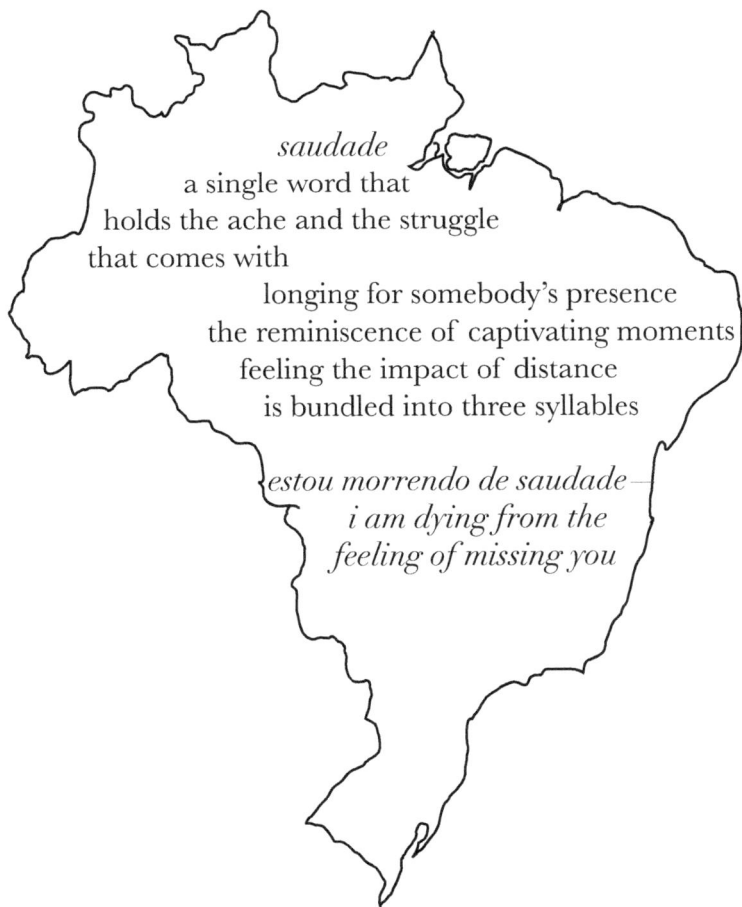

saudade
a single word that
holds the ache and the struggle
that comes with
longing for somebody's presence
the reminiscence of captivating moments
feeling the impact of distance
is bundled into three syllables

estou morrendo de saudade—
i am dying from the
feeling of missing you

solstice

some only care because they view it as an obligation
they will seem deplorable if they do not at least attempt
to feign interest
they must at the very least exhibit their new sets
of premedidated fibs

are you okay? they ask

the most orthodox question of them all
after you brought up the courage within yourself
to vent and cry and close your eyes
because your senses were far too fragile to handle what
the earth has provided you with

when was the last time they asked on their own accord?
your presence should be enough to make them care

laura lyrio

we are brought up like parrots
        mimicking what the outside world says
and learning to think that it is okay

solstice

ironic how group chats have a way of magnifying
the mundane

(if you want the spotlight)

like a snake sheds its skin
i set forth in pursuit of a new self

the image of a snake tends to be unfavorable
representing a false sense of sincerity
a traitor and a snitch
the friend of judas

yet a snake merely sheds because it has grown
and no longer fits the mold its old skin demands
it needs to be set free from the parasites that have latched
and the harsh constraints that have been bestowed

you never took the time to understand

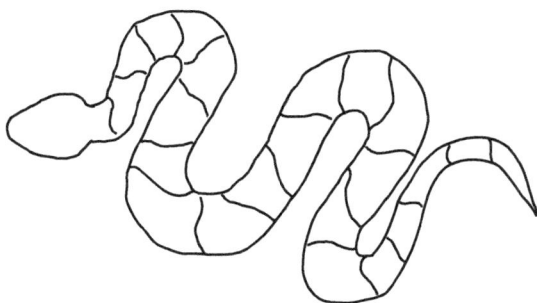

solstice

i become rather nauseous when asked if i am okay
a) depression and anxiety are quite fond of me
b) need i say more to validate my case?
i understand it comes with good intentions
but you should understand something too
no matter how much i try to explain or write
nothing will ever come close to being able to convey
how i think and rationalize
how i feel and process
and on those horrid days where nothing in my life seems
to be in place
my mind accepts that if nobody is able to understand me
nobody will be able to love me
and that frightens the hell out of me

now i have painted you a picture:
asking if i am okay
will lead me to believe that i am destined to end up alone

                    now do you understand
                    that you will never understand?

sometimes i lay on cotton carpets and hardwood floors
in hopes that the ground will swallow me entirely
no questions asked and no judgement passed
there will be nothing left separating me from the earth
i will simply become it

solstice

i go to the supermarket when i feel unloved
its aisles are the only things that still
light up at my presence

laura lyrio

i hope to learn the difference
between those who care
and those who thrive off curiosity

¿estás solamente chismeando?

solstice

it has been a rough couple of weeks for me i complained
everything happens for a reason you said
yet i beg to differ
what happens in life is the result of our own choices
actions have consequences and we somehow
mistake them for coincidences or an undeserving fate
if you were to believe that everything does happen for a
reason
you are claiming that we have a predestined fate
if that is so
what is the point in trying at all
if nothing we do will change the results?
why would we try if it does not matter?

your body is not a welcome mat
do not allow sleazy men
to overstep their stay

(adieu)

solstice

you cannot know beauty without
                                  hardship
you cannot know comfort without
                                  pain
you cannot know peace without
                                  danger
you cannot know hope without
                                  fear

one thing i feel i won't ever be able to comprehend is that
we are given a choice to either create or destroy
in a world that plants opportunities into sacred ground
and provides until it may begin to blossom at our very feet
yet we lift our legs and crush away the flourishing bundle
of the possibilities and positive choices we are offered
we replace chances given to us with devilish carelessness
and we feign dismay so that we may not have to deal with
the consequences we chose to take on

(we would rather lie than grow)

solstice

social media depicts a happy relationship
to be in accordance with grand gestures
teachers promote the ideology that a crush
innocently begins with a boy's insults
so we as women learn to live in a world of fragility
where the insults he spits at two fourteen in the morning
are uniform to love
and the flowers he bought earlier overcompensate
the fact he's been drinking
we accept the truths spoken because we never
fathomed that we were allowed to feel like we
deserve better
instead we wipe away the tears
and mumble to ourselves
it's okay, i know he loves me

laura lyrio

consent should never be swallowed
by impolite men
who hunger for more
than what they are offered

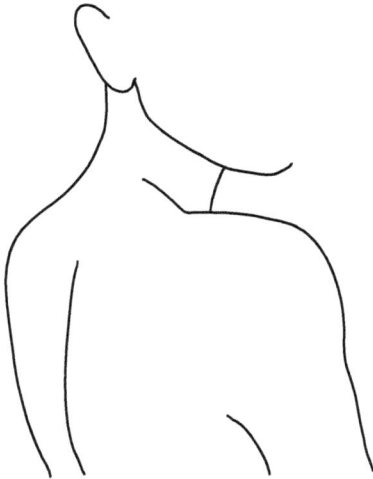

solstice

i like to believe that i do not hold much anger
within me
because anger is an overpowering emotion
and i prefer to be in control over what i feel
but
that day was an exception
where through tears and breakdowns
you made it known to me that you were
touched
and
invaded
without consent and
without ever wanting to be
my heart ached for you
my blood boiled

we now live in a society where
young girls are afraid and embarrassed to
 stand up for themselves
because of the repercussions and blame that follow
we no longer understand that we are all fragile
this is something that leaves mental and physical wounds
something that pushes away all true connections
something that results in overwhelming nightmares and
constant fear

whether we like to admit it or not
we instill this notion into women
that they won't be taken seriously
the man will never face
the punishments he deserves and so
he continues to live his life thinking it is okay

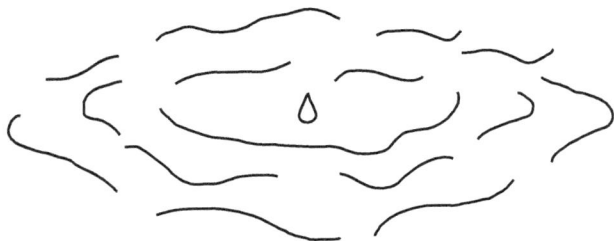

solstice

who i choose to love
is personal sentiment

how i choose to love
is public knowledge

do not confuse
what i allow you to know
with what you think you see

like a dragon slavers its truth with words of fire
you spit hot insults into my hands as if i
were nothing more than your inferior
i believed i would remain reserved without
your blazing warmth
yet when i brought up my hands to shield my eyes from
your slander
my eyes burned
and the only thing that dulled the pain were my own tears

it was through bitter self shattering that i realized i myself
could do all i thought i needed from you

solstice

i saw you and i knew
that you would break me without meaning to
and after continuously seeking advice
i came to find that all everyone seemed to say was
there is no way you can know for sure
i could not argue with that
so i allowed myself to become bound to him
and to care more about him than i should have:
i allowed myself to feel

how stupid can one girl be?

laura lyrio

you texted me every day for two years straight
and loved me on every single one of them
sometimes i cry because i
will never be able to understand
why we don't have a say in who we fall for

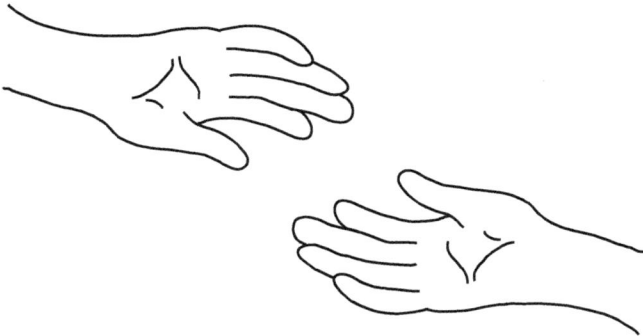

(r)

solstice

if you believe the book is better than the movie
or that the first is better than the sequel
how is it that you believe
that attempting a relationship with the same boy
will be better the second time?

there will come a time where the first rose petal will fall
i cannot help but wonder

if

you

will

stay

solstice

it's one seventeen in the morning
and your phone lights up
naturally your heart does too
its beats in sync with the vibrations
you receive one text
you have been expecting
for hours
if not days
from a person you know
is not good for you
(how long did it take
to repair yourself the last time?)
yet you convince yourself
that it will
somehow
someway
be different this time

you pick up your phone
and stare at the blue bubble
your fingers ache to move
you are left with a choice

choose yourself

laura lyrio

i realize it might be a stretch
it has been months and you live
on the other side of the world
there have been plenty girls since i imagine

but on sleepless nights
those where the pillow is no longer cold from
turning it over one too many times
and every plausible sleeping position is unfitting
i am left with no choice but to think
if you might still see me the way i see you

solstice

i don't care about the same things i used to
i don't think you don't realize that yet
you've always been too egocentric to see

what's always been in front of you

laura lyrio

my heart gnaws at my ribcage
not because i miss him
but because there is no longer
anything left
for me to hold on to

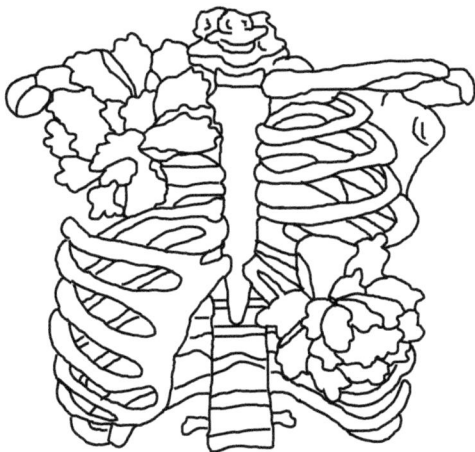

solstice

how ironic it is that
the only thing
that distinguishes
a part from apart
is space

you are a natural disaster:
unpredictable destructibility
from whom i seek refuge

solstice

call me murphy:
when it comes to me
if something can go wrong
i promise it will

(even the law itself)

laura lyrio

please i said
my own words were breaking me
don't

(the things we hide)

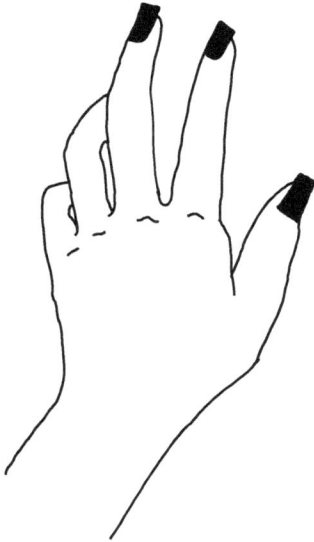

solstice

i know not everything is about me
but i have cried every day this week
and it is far too late to ask for reasons
you saw the signs and chose to ignore
them
do not lie to me
that was your choice
      now it is time i make mine

laura lyrio

you always had a fascination with records
sadistically admiring how they played music for you
when they were scratched
each song attempting to serenade you more than the other
how you admired their willingness to hurt for you
with every sound came a hint of enthrallment and soon
the symphony you created mesmerized every cell in my body
i longed to provide you with the same satisfaction as them
after all they played their music beautifully
the damage caused was a mere side effect
nothing in comparison to the goddess i thought myself to be
you played me and i mistook it for endearment

solstice

when his hands gently stroked my back
and his thumb drew circles on my palms
my head between his collarbones and neck
i felt happy
so it was
in that moment
i came to terms with my own truth
it would not last
i would soon ruin it like i do everything else
and that is all it would ever be
i broke it off a few days later
as i had done with all those who came before

and then i ask *why*
why is it that i can never stick to anyone
i am incapable of understanding my patterns
is there something wrong with me?

you ruin things because you fear them she sighed
you fear the possibility of someone loving you
since you never learned to love yourself

laura lyrio

my eyes are a rainforest
water never stops
f
a
l
l
i
n
g

(yet flowers bloom)

solstice

we rely on a muscle that pumps our blood
to make decisions too fragile to be made with the mind
so tell me again
how is it possible to not allow our emotions cloud our
judgement
when the same blood we associate with our feelings
flows within our rational mind?

looking at you was like studying light
beautiful but blinding
my senses dulled with each discreet glance
and in time you were the one thing in my line of vision
you were the brightest thing i had ever seen
i dreamt of the day i would be too
day after day i stared more and more
blinding myself
in hopes that if i soaked you in like the sun
maybe you would notice me

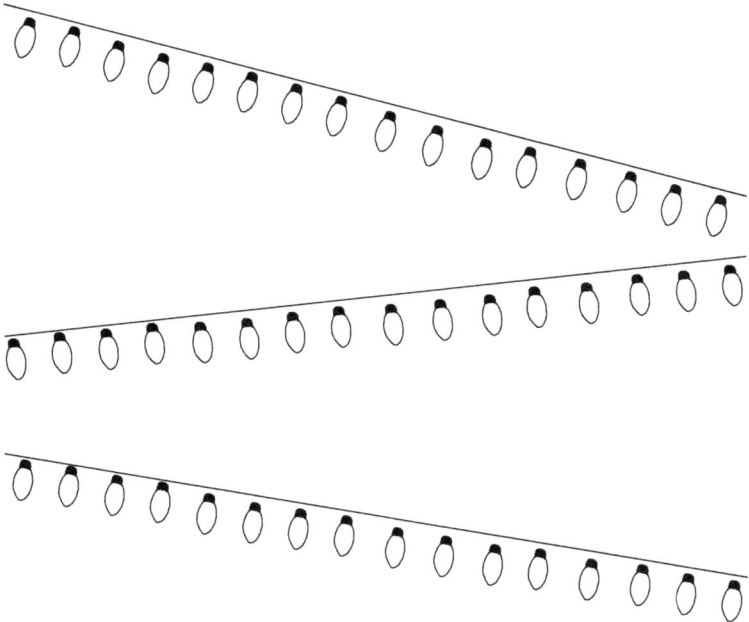

summer
solstice

"the sun travels the longest path through the sky, and that day therefore has the most daylight and the longest day"

your calloused fingers unfastened
to display the most captivating
magnificence which extended an invitation
to explore the mysteries that laid beneath your palm

(a love affair with your hands)

solstice

he is a question mark
and i a mere period
he is ambiguously shaped
differs in perspective
nonetheless still needed always curious
never final
and me
just a speck
a minuscule hard punch
and that is all
yet i am still a part of him
he still needs me
every time you search for him
i will be there

(punctuation)

wake up but take your time
the day outside arises early
inside the day passes ever so slowly
but i never regret spending this time with you

solstice

you follow paths you never knew existed
and deeply explore unknown cities
one hand on the wheel one hand on her thigh
you play by the rules yet still there are
head on collisions

(traffic and love)

laura lyrio

i will follow you
as sunflowers do the sun
your warmth engulfs me

(haiku #1)

solstice

it was four ten in the morning
i had a smile on my face that moved muscles
i never knew i had
yet my entire body was hit with an overwhelming sense
of pain
i dislike the distance but i like you more

(d)

laura lyrio

just as the leaves that settle in hot tea
your love kept me rooted
and every time i believed there was no more
for you to soak up
your intensity flourished so that
that every time i felt that i was not enough
you would remind me of my strength
we were great separately that is true
but we had a warm, flavorful kind of love
thank you for making me more than i was

solstice

the sun sets in tiny miracles
life is composed of the same combinations of dull colors
but the sun on the west pushes colors to transform into
shades the naked eye has never seen before
stringy purplish pink clouds spread across the horizon
resembling a bottomless jar of sweet cotton candy
the sky resembles a mixture of the ocean and the sky
a world of blues mixing together in perfect harmony
each blue is a happy hugh because
it is the only time the dark can unite with the light
the dark colors say hello and the light waves goodbye
the sun becomes smaller and smaller
each ray of orange and red revolving around each other
fighting for dominance
and the colors reflect onto ponds and oceans
mimicking the perfection across its terrestrial counterpart
sunlight spreads among the grass
urging the lonesome threads to soak in the vivid rays
the colors of the sky begin to fight for what seems like
forever but are only minutes
but eventually the dark outweighs the light
so it must leave but does so ever so slowly
as if savoring each and every moment

there will always be these few minutes
where we focus on the sky above
to distract ourselves from the problems below

laura lyrio

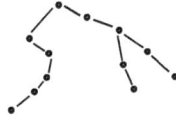

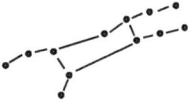

you light me up brighter than the stars
and form constellations with my smile
you free me like gravity
yet i still fall for you

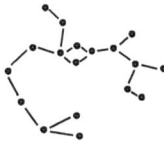

solstice

we were parallel lines
never talking never touching
but very similar
how i longed to become familiar with you
but we were on different planes
so we extended infinitely
in our set places
never moving never meeting
yet i knew we were the same

laura lyrio

like every great cartographer implements a fake city
onto their map
i created a city never meant to exist within you
we were not meant to be together
yet we were
defying all the universal laws of balance
ever so slowly that city flourished so intricately
that it became real
and when the universe finally decided we could no longer be
i was not worried
for i knew my city would remain within you always

(summer stories)

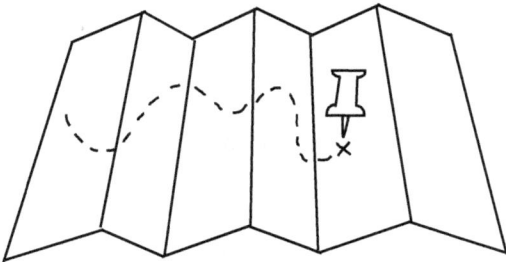

you're just too much
are the last words i remember you professing
with prostration in your eyes
so i vowed to become less for you
maybe you would love me again
day by day i shaved off more parts of myself
bit by bit i became less whole
until finally all that was left were dusty remains
of what once was
i was ready for you
to be loved by you
yet you denied me without the slightest
acknowledgement of what i had done
day by day i became more weary
bit by bit i fell apart
my true colors had vanished and all that
remained were pigments
i could not even hate myself for the atrocities
i performed
because there was nothing left of me to hate
that was before i met you
day by day we became more intertwined
bit by bit you helped me heal
and in time
the pigments that remained transformed into
watercolors

laura lyrio

you say my name like it belongs somewhere
but not just anywhere—
a place that tranforms whispers into songs
where heavenly fire burns away
the sins that brought us there
yet we commit them all the same
and from your lips drip my name
gold plated and all
your hands on my cheek tell me
all i need to know

solstice

your touch feels like ice
somehow i crave you more

(beneath the surface)

laura lyrio

i remember
waiting for you on the last of eight days
on the top wooden floor
your arm clutching your elbow
your accent thicker than usual
you felt like
home and vacation bundled neatly into one
we walked hand brushing hand at two in the morning
the ocean beneath us
the stars above us
the lights twinkling
you looked at me as if you were afraid to break me
afraid that touching me would be like a sugar cube
dissolving under your warm touch
no boy had ever looked at me like that before
(and no boy has ever since)
you took the risk you went for it
and boy
am i glad that you did

(te echo de menos)

solstice

we stayed up til 4
laughter ringing through the phone
cheek on my pillow
a wide smile across my face
oh how i wish you lived here

(tanka #1)

laura lyrio

his foreign dialect
transforms words into sugar
melting away into the abyss
thick like maple syrup
sweet the same way
his beautiful country
resides in his tongue

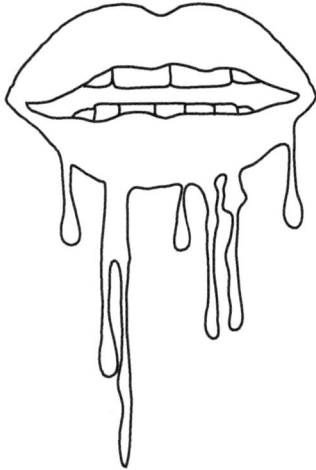

my fingertips roamed the bag for the green flavored candy
(i know it is your favorite too)
i sat cross-legged and allowed the cold to seep through my
legs
i laughed unbelievably hard
it reopened a chamber of secrets within me
forgotten by the past
unknown to the future
i glanced at you to find you staring at me
within me
my red cheeks became rose petals
and the words tumbled
where would i be without you
as i said it i realized
it was not a matter of where i would be
but rather if i
would want to be
here
without you

laura lyrio

in seconds you were able to give me what i have
longed for
but could not provide myself with
your absence

(thank you for doing what i could not)

solstice

the warmth consumes me
it is the taste of coffee
that enriches me

(haiku #2)

laura lyrio

we are all capable of providing the world with
the love it so desperately needs
yet we prefer to hold grudges and to
deny our own mistakes
learn to concede to the universe so it may plant
its seeds of kindness within you
choose to nurture and care for it so that it may one day
blossom into the beauty it was meant to become
and once you have been saved by your own actions
allow your heart to enclose the world with gardens
that will bloom relentlessly because of you

solstice

a year went by and i had not heard from you
yet all it took was a five second picture
for me to feel just as i did when i first met you

things are far from where they once were
to be honest i still don't know what went wrong
i should have tried harder
done something
i am sorry

i know life has not been so kind to you
but i love you more than you could ever know
i hope you know that

(s)

laura lyrio

bruises the color of roses
thighs as thick as trees
stretch marks made of lightning
freckles as sporadic as stars

(you are made of earth)

solstice

seeds survive in a mere dormant state
patiently awaiting renewal
and even then
barely alive
the only way they may come to life
to grow and to flourish is to be
buried
deep down below in damp soil
so much pressure for one little seedling to handle
despite all odds it does
it pushes and pushes and pushes
it pushes so hard that a root manages to branch out
and then another one
and suddenly it has claimed its territory
ignoring improbabilities it continues upwards this time
it pushes and pushes and pushes
until it becomes a mis-matched mosaic
composed of delicate petals and colored leaves

if a seed can do it
why can't you?

(despite the odds)

laura lyrio

i just can't help but think that bad things keep
happening to me i said

have you ever thought of the ocean she said
how there are smaller waves and bigger ones
you'll become engulfed if you ever take them head on
but
if you stand on your side
you'll stand a better chance
you'll take it on the same
yet
the impact won't be as bad
you can overcome it
so be the ocean
tackle your problems on your side

(thank you mrs. blanco)

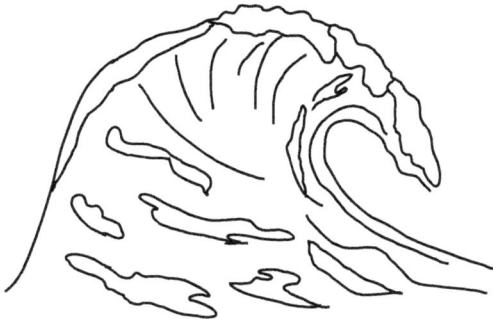

solstice

listen because we have been screaming
but your repulsive fingers lay steadily on our mouths
not trembling because we know better
any sign of weakness will be held against us
when did innocent until proven guilty
become only applicable to those in power
respect your elders they say
i scoff
age does not gain you respect nor
does it prevent you from acquiring it
respect must be earned
have faith in yourself and so will the rest of us
your heart
can and will change the world

laura lyrio

we have become so accustomed to having information at
our fingertips
that when more complex matters come to hand
the world can no longer think for itself
it cannot take responsibility for its own actions
it becomes
my parents say my friends think the internet suggests

nature has provided us with complex minds
from which intricate thought originate
yet we take advantage and act dumbfounded

it is time for you to stand up for your beliefs your opinions
your values your passions
it is your voice that will change the world
not your parents' not your friends' not the internet's
be confident and act true to yourself

you and i are the future

solstice

with awareness comes action
not one session went by without the utterance
of those elementary words
and with the simplicity came the lesson of a lifetime:
all it takes is the understanding of a situation
within yourself for

you

to enact change

i am so tired of the excuses and demotivation
the you can'ts and the what ifs
i just need one single
go for it
who knows
our ideas might just change the world

(all we need are people who believe in us)

solstice

you see, my love
you have no say in what happens to you
but you can control how you react
the time you waste pining over what could have been
is the time you lose to make what could be
do not cry, my dear
for life goes on to give you gifts you never knew
you could wish for

(p)

i chose the little stand instead of the lavish one
(so of course it was quite empty)
a man sat on a stool choosing threads for his next creation
the woman gently waved and then smiled
she began to walk away but i called her back
you made these i said *so tell me which are your favorites*
she looked taken aback but placed in my hand
an elephant, a figure of buddha, and an ohm sign
i smiled and told her i would take all three
she intercepted and said *now you get one free*
in turn i asked her husband *which is your favorite*
he ignored me but continued working with his hands
his wife told me to wait before i chose another
and so i did
this is my favorite flower, a lotus he said
he rolled up his sleeve and showed me the image tattooed
on his arm
it is the epitomic symbol of wisdom
puzzled i asked why it wasn't on display like the rest
with smiling eyes the phrase rolled off his tongue
wisdom is only obtainable to those who seek it

solstice

sending handwritten letters to
articulate our most intricate thoughts on
the unknown and the things we fear are
too real to say aloud
i become old-fashioned for our friendship

(k)

it began with a water bottle
(who knew it would become one of the most influential
moments of my life)
ever since it has been a consistent balance between
coffee and grades and family stories
summer stories and internship essays
anxiety and breakdowns and motivation

it is because we have been labeled and outcasted
that God put us in each other's path
it is you who has given me the strength to continue
who motivates me when i feel i am worth close to nothing
it is you who has shaped me into the courageous
(and psychotic)
person i am today
thank you

(e)

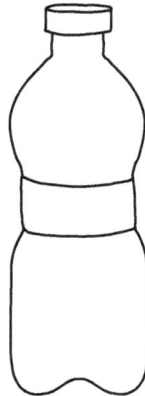

solstice

tenho saudades do que nunca aconteceu

laura lyrio

the boundaries between our
bones break because we were
bound to be together

solstice

the greatest compliment i have ever been paid
was that i seemingly have been blessed with an
understanding beyond thought
and that i will never forget

(thank you mrs. diaz)

just because there is a finish line
doesn't mean you have to imagine
what it will look like when you cross it

solstice

i must learn to come to terms with acceptance
over the things beyond my reach
there are commodities that must simply
be left in the hands of God
but
if there is even a minuscule chance for change
you are damned if you think
i won't do all that i can
to ensure what i seek

laura lyrio

not everyone enjoys cinnamon
i find it irresistible
sweet and savory all at once
rich in flavor and in health
a peppery pungent warmth

i like it
and to me
that is enough

(self actualization)

solstice

i am who i am
and i do all that i can do
maybe it won't be enough for everyone
but to myself
i know i am worth it
i am not confined by
my test scores or colleges i apply to
i am not limited to
the pictures of me on social media

my validity is defined by the love around me

laura lyrio

elle attend comme un livre qui veut être lu

(pour madame suarez)

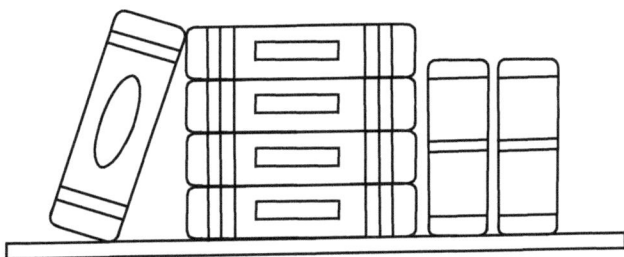

solstice

i stayed because i thought you brought out the best in me
until i realized
the best of me had always been there
you awakened me and i am strong enough
to say goodbye

with achey steps and shaky breaths
i stood down before you and apologized
for crimes i never commit because
you made me feel guilty over your own actions
you deceived me into believing you were a
savior coming to redeem me
because you were simply that good
so you smiled down at me and proceeded to
tell me i was nothing to you
i stood up and walked away
without seeing your face
i could sense the outrage radiating from you
yet i knew the battle was won

there is only so much you can do for a person
put yourself first

solstice

so many times i've thought about giving up and ending it all
it wasn't until i came across a picture that asked me
if you had ended your life yourself last year
what great things would you have missed out on?

this poem
is for you to finish

laura lyrio

i covered my bedroom wall in four hundred distinct pictures
each resembling a person a place a memory a feeling
and at times
when numbness strikes
and the feeling (or lack therefore)
becomes more than i can bear
with shallow breaths and spacious steps
i walk backwards until i hit the wall opposite the images
and allow myself to be engrossed in them
enabling my eyes and brain to remember and accept
everything and everyone
to hit me at once
how much life has changed and how it continues to do so
this i tell myself
this is how you fix yourself
let yourself remember

solstice

i am undeservingly loved by the one true God

who waters my soul with adam's ale
as a reminder that the mistakes committed before me
do not define who i am but guide me to truth

who provides me with a hideaway in prayer
as a reminder that He will always be home and
provide even when we may not understand

who paints me into a unique mosaic
as a reminder that the person i was created to be is
unparalleled
the colors that make me were pensively painted

and for this i thank you

laura lyrio

if the love isn't sacrificial,
it's artificial

(thank you mr. cabrera)

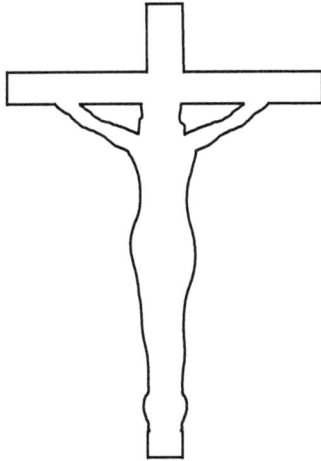

solstice

what took me sixteen years to learn i pass along to you:
to surround yourself with positive energy
-it spreads like wildfire
to smile and be kind to the world around you
-even if it is not so kind to you
to take naps that reawaken your juvenile self
-the world is tiring after all
it is important to disregard the things that make you
uncomfortable
-never give in to what is not you
to aim your focus on your future and not your past
-you can only move forward
to endorse yourself in life's simple pleasures
-face masks and books and cookies
there is a difference between being selfish and practicing
self care
treat yourself kindly and the world will too

(patricia's lessons)

there will always be people who don't like you
for whatever the reasons may be
instead of allowing it to consume you
realize all you have to do is
love yourself a little more
to make up for it

(self love)

solstice

my life was never the same after you
i was a late bloomer
but you managed to help me blossom
you made me look beautiful

(thank you a)

who knew that a three day retreat could change my
perception of life
after countless days of being lost within myself
wanting to change the world but not knowing how
not being able to say
i
love
you
to the mirror's portrayal of myself
i was suddenly transported to the world which relied
solely on kairos time
and the recognition of not only the imperfections
but perfections
within myself
and after a mere three days
not only did i not hesitate in saying those three words to
myself
but i was able to accept myself just as i am
i have never felt so empowered

what is duke tip? is a question i get so frequently
and i still don't know how to answer
it was around mid december
when my parents told me i was taking the college sat
to get into a summer camp that would teach me how to live
as almost no 13 year old would, i dreamt of the day
i took it with confidence, didn't study
but there was something about seeing my middle school self
surrounded by high schoolers
and scoring higher than most of them
that gave myself hope
and in the summer of 2015
i went to rollins, my home
but it wasn't until two years later at uga
where i would find for myself the true meaning of family
tip is the place where 49 other weeks don't matter because
the 3 you get are your world
it's the place where you go to learn because you want to
because you are smart
because you are capable
because everyone around you believes in you
tip is the reason you say "everywhere" when someone asks
where your friends are
and they become so much more than that
they become your family
you become close to the people you promised yourself
you'd never talk to
and they turn your entire life around

tip is the place you think about when someone tells you to
smile
it's the place where no one will judge you for crying when
a song plays at a dance
it's the place where your only identity is your lanyard
you are free to be who you choose to, and love without
question
tip is my instinctive reply when someone asks my where
home is
it's the place where everyone cares about you no matter
who you are or what you do
tip will forever and always
be my home
uga
will forever and always
be my home
so what do i answer to that most simple question?
it's easy.
"tip is love."

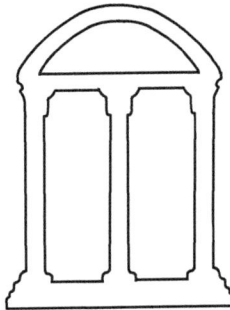

solstice

there will come a time where
the girl who went to the bookstore for the
simple joy it brought her
curled up in a corner with coffee in one hand and
a book in the other
will become
the woman who visits bookstores across the country
coffee still in hand
and makes people smile with her words
because she will be the one
writing them

my name is laura lyrio caram
i am altruistic but impetuous
i love my friends with all the love my heart can carry
i am thankful for all the sadness i've had to endure
(i would have never learned if not for that)
my family lives in another country
but not a day goes by when they are not on my mind
i like to light candles and listen to my sleepy time playlist
i think coffee is the greatest thing to ever exist
i enjoy reading books that take me to another life when
my own is not so great
my favorite thing to think about are the stars and the
undiscovered universe
and most importantly
writing gives me purpose

(an ending)

do me a favor before you go. think of a house. now imagine yourself building that house with everyone you know. what would happen if everyone decided to work on the same wall, and nothing else? would the house ever finish being built? or what if one single screw was missing? would the house be able to stand still perfectly on its own? now think of the house as the world around you. life could not go on if everyone were to be the same. nothing would ever get done. it is our differences that make it possible to create. and without your gifts, the world would be missing an essential piece of it. the world needs you to go on. you are here for a purpose. never doubt your abilities or accomplishments. never doubt your worth. you are here. even though you may wish otherwise. power through. it will be worth it. that is my promise, from me to you.

(acknowledgements)

i would like to begin by saying that i immensely appreciate everyone who took the time to read this book. i could have never imagined this for myself—a self-published author at merely seventeen. you are what helped make this possible for me.

there are many people i would like to thank for helping with and inspiring the very book you hold in your hands. to my family: thank you to my mom (paula caram), dad (antonio caram), and sister (sophia caram) for tolerating my deep remarks, loud music, and sporadic personality but choosing to love me despite it all. thank you to the entirety of my family in brasil, but especially my grandparents (luiz lirio, sandra lirio, antonio caram, angela caram), my aunt (patricia lyrio), my uncle (guillerme lirio), and my cousins (arthur samora and matheus samora), for continuing to be the greatest support system i could ever ask for even from thousands of miles away. thank you to my childhood friends turned family, luiza marson and giovanna basso, for sticking with me and always encouraging me to be the best i can be.

to my friends: thank you to all the beautiful people who attended duke tip at uga term 2 (especially maya offir, jack gillis, summer sun, ashley amontree, and willa buresh) because you made me who i am today;

all of you reside in me and i am forever grateful. thank you to ava solorzano, sophia pargas, emily salado, and sabrina barnola for never failing to love and believe in me and for holding my hand when i need it most. thank you to sebastian betancourt, anthony alonso, and matias ayesta for continuously encouraging me and for the constant support and belief in me. special thank you to my best friend, esteban rincon for never giving up on me and for teaching me that the friendships you never see coming become the most impactful.

most importantly, thank you to every person who has been a part of my story. my life has not always been the easiest, but you all gave me something to write about— you provided me with an escape. it takes both good and bad to grow, and once you learn to accept that, life will become far easier. there will always be people who don't necessarily love what you do, so you learn to love yourself a little more to make up for it.

never allow anybody to tell you what you can and cannot do. at the end of the day, you yourself hold the key that unlocks your future. do not let it go to waste seeking permission and approval. take your life into your own hands and do what makes you happy. who knows, you might surprise yourself. sending love and blessings your way.

www.ingramcontent.com/pod-product-compliance
Lightning Source LLC
Chambersburg PA
CBHW060022050426
42448CB00012B/2842

* 9 7 8 0 5 7 8 5 4 8 0 5 0 *